PIONEERS IN HEALTH AND MEDICINE

The Life of

Daniel Hale Williams

Judith Kaye

Twenty-First Century Books

A Division of Henry Holt and Company New York

PHOTO CREDITS
pages 4, 40, 61, and 67: Schomburg Center for Research in Black Culture/NYPL. **page 24:** Galter Health Sciences Library, Northwestern University, Chicago. **page 30:** Chicago Historical Society. **page 55:** D.H. Williams Papers, Box 116-125, Folder 22, Manuscripts Division, Moorland-Spingarn Research Center, Howard University. **page 76:** Smithsonian Institution, Photo No. 67045.

Twenty-First Century Books
A Division of Henry Holt and Company, Inc.
115 West 18th Street
New York, NY 10011

Published in Canada by Fitzhenry & Whiteside Ltd., 195 Allstate Parkway, Markham, Ontario L3R 4T8

Library of Congress Cataloging-in-Publication Data
Kaye, Judith
The Life of Daniel Hale Williams / Judith Kaye. — 1st ed.
p.   cm. — (Pioneers in Health and Medicine)
Includes index.
Summary: A biography of the African-American doctor who performed the first surgery on the human heart in the nineteenth century and who founded the first interracial hospital in the United States.
1. Williams, Daniel Hale, 1856-1931—Juvenile literature.
2. Afro-American surgeons—Biography—Juvenile literature.
3. Surgeons—United States—Biography—United States.
[1. Williams, Daniel Hale, 1856-1931. 2. Physicians.
3. Afro-Americans—Biography.] I. Title. II. Series.
RD27.35.W54K38 1993
617'.092—dc20   [B]   93-7986   CIP   AC

ISBN 0-8050-2302-x
First Edition—1993

Printed in the United States of America
All first editions are printed on acid-free paper ∞.
10 9 8 7 6 5 4 3 2 1

Contents

Dr. Daniel Hale Williams

1

Brawler's Knife, Surgeon's Knife

Chicago's summer of 1893 was hot. The nights seemed long, and tempers were often short. Fights broke out on the playgrounds, on the streets, and in the bars. The staff at Provident Hospital had no reason to be surprised when a young man was rushed in with a knife wound in his chest. No one expected that this patient would go down in medical history.

At first, James Cornish's wound did not seem very serious. There was little bleeding. The knife seemed to have been plunged in, then withdrawn cleanly. The cut, between the fourth and fifth ribs on the left side, was only about an inch wide. However, no one knew how long the knife's blade had been.

Cornish was in pain and was showing signs of weakening. Soon the staff called in "Dr. Dan," the young black doctor who, just two years before, had founded this small interracial hospital. Dr. Daniel Hale Williams was highly respected for his skill as a surgeon. The doctors attending Cornish wanted Williams to have a look at this wound.

Dr. Dan checked the patient's pulse and temperature, looked at his skin and his eyes, and watched him breathe. He saw that Cornish's condition was not good. However, the area around the wound gave the doctor few clues about why. Something was wrong inside this wounded man. The question was what.

In those days, there were no X-rays, no sonograms, no CAT scans or MRIs. Doctors in the late nineteenth century had few of the tools that doctors use today to find out what is happening inside a diseased or wounded body. Dr. Williams decided to wait and keep a close watch.

Daniel Williams went back to his office and hung up his white jacket. He was thin, graceful, neat, and well groomed from his shoes to his carefully trimmed mustache. Now Dr. Williams sat down to read medical and administrative reports from the large pile on his desk. He was prepared to remain for the night, if necessary, to help his patient.

From time to time, Dr. Williams interrupted his reading to check on Cornish. Clearly the patient was failing, but there was still no clue as to what was causing the problem.

Daniel Williams had seen patients with deep knife wounds before. He knew they often bled internally and too often died. A knife wound in the left side of the chest might go near, or even into, the heart. Heart wounds were usually fatal. In the 1890s, doctors did not try to mend internal damage. The standard procedure was simply to keep patients with chest wounds cool and quiet, and hope the body would heal itself.

Doctors had good reasons to avoid operations in which they would open up the body. Internal bleeding was difficult to control, and blood transfusions were not yet known. The danger of infection was great, and antibiotics to fight infections had not yet been invented. The use of anesthetics to control pain was new and risky.

Under such conditions, a surgeon had to make decisions and use his instruments quickly. These were exactly the skills for which Dr. Dan was famous. Like most surgeons of his time, though, Williams had operated mostly on arms and legs or near the surface of the body—dealing with infected areas, performing amputations, and removing small growths.

The problems caused by James Cornish's knife wound lay deep inside the body, and the situation was getting worse. By morning, Dr. Williams felt he must do something or the man would die. With little information or experience to guide him in safely and effectively opening up a human chest, Daniel Williams decided to operate.

Williams sent word to several doctors he knew would want to witness this operation. He made sure the operating room was scoured until it was completely clean. Then he scrubbed his hands and arms thoroughly.

As Dr. Williams began to cut into Cornish's chest, he had one great advantage over many doctors of his time. He had studied human anatomy carefully. Still, anatomy only told him what the chest cavity should look like—not about the damage done by a knife inside this particular body.

The operation began. Dr. Williams rapidly sliced through skin, then flesh, then cartilage. The small room became hot and stuffy as the six watching doctors and the surgical nurses crowded in. Finally, Dr. Dan could see what threatened his patient's life. The point of the knife blade had pierced the heart itself.

Williams had been aware of the dangers in performing this operation—and not only for his patient. Cornish was likely to die whether Williams operated or not. If the operation was the direct cause of death, the reputation of young Provident Hospital, and of Dr. Daniel Hale Williams, its founder, would suffer.

But James Cornish did not die. The operation—the first successful operation on the human heart—was the most famous surgery Daniel Williams performed in a long, busy, and productive life.

That one dramatic operation has sometimes overshadowed Dr. Williams's other accomplishments. Williams, the son of a barber, was a free black born just before the Civil War. He struggled long and hard to get a good education for himself. From 1883, when he opened his practice, until long after he retired from Provident Hospital in 1912, Daniel Hale Williams made history in three major areas.

First, Daniel Williams was a great surgeon whose work had enormous influence on the practice of surgery. He was a teaching doctor who could keep up his commentary and explanation while he was cutting into and mending a patient's ailing body. By both instruction and example he influenced many other surgeons to attempt operations that had seldom, if ever, been performed before.

Second, Dr. Williams was a great builder of institutions. He founded Provident Hospital in Chicago because African Americans in the nineteenth century had little access to quality hospital care. He also rebuilt Freedmen's Hospital, a government hospital in Washington, D.C., turning it into a first-class institution after years of neglect.

Third, by establishing programs to employ black interns and train black nurses, Daniel Hale Williams made great strides in opening the field of medicine to African Americans.

Even after he retired from hospital work, Daniel Williams continued to teach and to work for the building of hospitals and medical colleges for blacks. Always he insisted on the highest standards of training and practice. And always he insisted that both patient beds and staff positions be open to people of all races.

2

The Early Years

Daniel Hale Williams was born on January 18, 1856, five years before the Civil War began. He was the fifth child of Daniel Williams, Jr., and Sarah Price Williams. Little Daniel's large and happy family included a brother and five sisters.

Daniel's father made a good living as a barber in the bustling town of Hollidaysburg, Pennsylvania. The town was at the head of the Pennsylvania State Canal, so many travelers came through needing a beard trimmed, a mustache shaped, or a face shaved. Mr. Williams also owned some property, which added to the family's prosperity.

Daniel's ancestors on both sides were a mixture of African American, Native American, and European. Some of them were farmers; others, like young Daniel's father, owned real estate and small businesses. Many of the Williamses and Prices, including both Daniel's grandfathers, were also preachers.

Young Daniel had fair skin, reddish-brown hair, and facial features that seemed to come from his Scotch-Irish and German ancestors. Some of his family were so light of skin that they had crossed the color line and were living as whites. But most members of both the Williams and Price families, including Daniel's mother and father, were proud to consider themselves African Americans.

Hollidaysburg was an important stop on the Underground Railroad that smuggled slaves out of the South to freedom. Many people on both sides of Daniel's family, including his father and his mother's cousin Frederick Douglass, worked to free the slaves and better the conditions of all blacks. The Williams children took a great interest in the issues of slavery and freedom.

Daniel had a pleasant life, playing with his brother and sisters, attending school, watching the comings and goings on the canal and on Hollidaysburg's busy streets, and helping in his father's barbershop. He was always welcome to come talk and to help keep the mugs, brushes, towels, razors, and scissors tidy and clean.

When Daniel was eleven, this happy family life suddenly ended. Soon after the Civil War, the family had gone for an extended visit to Mrs. Williams's family in Annapolis, Maryland. From there, Mr. Williams began to travel for the National Equal Rights League, which was working for full freedom and citizenship for all African Americans. Mr. Williams exhausted himself with constant travel and many speeches, and he developed consumption, which we now call tuberculosis. After one particularly difficult trip, he returned home sick and never recovered.

His father left Daniel several important legacies: the skill of barbering; memories of working together; the commitment to make things better for his people; and some words that Dan remembered for the rest of his life: "Get all the education you can. We colored people must cultivate the mind."

Mr. Williams's death left his wife brokenhearted and unable to cope. She had married at fifteen, and her husband had always handled all business matters and money. Now she did not know how to manage the property and investments he had left, or how to care for their children.

Dan's brother, Price, who was twenty, decided to go to Philadelphia to study law. When the two oldest sisters were invited by some of their father's cousins to move to Rockford, Illinois, where they could study hairdressing and how to make false hairpieces and hair jewelry, Mrs. Williams decided to go with them. She sent two of the younger girls to an expensive boarding school in Baltimore, Maryland, and arranged for Grandmother Price to care for the youngest daughter. His mother decided that Daniel, who would need to earn his own living when he grew up, should learn shoemaking from an old family friend who ran a small training school in his Baltimore home.

Daniel's life changed completely. Without the comfort and security of a loving family, he was forced, at age eleven, to begin to make the decisions that formed the course of his life. He was on his own.

Daniel's first decision was to leave the shoemaker. Dan was fond of the man and didn't mind hard work, but he did not like making shoes. Within months, he followed his mother to Rockford. Mrs. Williams laughed when he arrived, Dan remembered years later, and commented that the trip showed he had the spunk to take care of himself.

Dan would need his spunk, for soon his mother moved back east. Daniel stayed in the West, with his sister Sally. The family, once close, was now permanently split. They kept up with each other by mail, but for years they rarely saw each other.

Dan and Sally moved frequently, taking what jobs they could find. Sally worked with hair. Daniel worked on boats on the Great Lakes and at barbering, first as an apprentice and later with a small shop of his own. He bought a guitar and, remembering chords his uncle had shown him in happier days, taught himself to play.

In 1873, when Dan was seventeen, he and Sally

found good jobs and settled in Janesville, Wisconsin, thirty miles north of Rockford. Janesville was in the Rock River valley, which had rich land for farming and water power for mills and manufacturing. Factories produced farm machinery, canned pickles, buggies, sleighs, and shoes. Janesville people were hard-working and proud of their industry, their town, and its commercial college.

Sally worked in hair goods, making artificial hairpieces and hair jewelry, and Dan took a job at Charles Henry Anderson's Tonsorial Parlor and Bathing Rooms. "Harry" Anderson had a prosperous, six-chair barbershop, which also provided baths for a population without indoor plumbing.

Harry Anderson—like Dan, a black of mixed blood—was delighted to find such an industrious, well-trained young barber. He and his wife, Ellen, an Irish immigrant, invited Dan and his sister to live in their home and treated them almost like their own children. Sally lived there until she married and moved farther north.

Dan enjoyed being part of a large family again. He often cared for, and played with, the Anderson children. The youngest child, born after Dan had been living with the family a few years, was named Daniel, after his godfather, Daniel Hale Williams.

In addition to his barbershop, Harry Anderson had a popular string band, which played at weddings, anniversaries, and dances and also accompanied traveling performers. When he found that Dan could play the guitar, Anderson encouraged him to learn the bass fiddle, too. Dan became a band regular. The twenty-piece group traveled around Wisconsin playing everything from square dance tunes to opera.

Daniel learned a lot from listening to the men who came to Harry Anderson's barbershop discuss news and argue about the issues of the day. Whenever business was slow, he jumped into a barber chair and read, preferably history or biography. He borrowed books from the Young Men's Association and from his customers. But Dan remembered his father's advice about getting a formal education. He wanted to go to school.

Daniel asked Harry Anderson to allow him to cut back on the hours he worked in the barbershop. He began studying at the Classical Academy, a private high school where, among other subjects, he learned the Latin and German that would prove useful for reading medical books. Although Dan spent most of his time studying, his reduced wages still covered the school fees: seventy-five cents a week.

Daniel apparently had not encountered much racism in his early life. His family, and the Andersons, lived prosperous middle-class lives, and Dan lived now in the West where relations between the races were less restricted than in the South and where quality seemed to count for more than heredity. Dan's light skin may also have spared him some insults and attacks.

But when Dan started going to the academy, the father of one of the other students objected to someone with "colored blood" attending the school. Other students and the principal immediately stood up for Dan, and the incident ended without trouble. Another situation, involving the parent of a white girl with whom Daniel danced frequently at academy dances, also came to nothing. Daniel continued to be a popular dance partner with girls his age, and he had many friends among his white classmates.

At twenty-one years of age, when Dan Williams finished his studies and graduated from the academy, he went back to working full time at the barbershop. He had gotten himself a good basic education, but he did not yet know how he wanted to use it.

3

Becoming a Doctor

Although Daniel enjoyed being a barber, he was eager to start planning some other path for his life. His brother, Price, now practicing law in Philadelphia, suggested that Daniel join him and train to become a lawyer.

Dan decided to follow his brother's suggestion, but without leaving Janesville. At that time, to become a lawyer a person studied law books and "read law" by serving a kind of apprenticeship in a lawyer's office. Dan signed on with a busy attorney but soon decided that he liked law no better than he had liked making shoes. Years later Dan explained that he didn't like law because lawyers made money out of people's arguments—and he had always hated arguments. He returned to the barbershop and the band, and kept reading whenever he had a chance.

The newspapers often carried lively accounts about one of the shop's customers, Dr. Henry Palmer, saving patients' lives. Dr. Palmer had been director of the largest military hospital during the Civil War and surgeon general of Wisconsin for ten years. He was now practicing medicine in Janesville, and he had a statewide reputation as an excellent doctor and a particularly fine surgeon.

Daniel always enjoyed hearing Dr. Palmer talk about his cases. One day, he found the courage to tell Dr. Palmer he was thinking of becoming a doctor.

Dr. Palmer looked hard at the young man. The doctor asked Dan if he could bear the sight of people in pain, of broken bodies, of sick children he could not cure. Dr. Palmer told Daniel about the long hours a doctor had to work and about riding through blizzards to reach the homes of patients who needed medical care. And there had been so many medical discoveries recently, the doctor said, that it was no longer possible to become a good doctor as people used to do when he himself began in medicine. Back then, a young person simply worked with a practicing physician until he knew what there was to know. Now, Dr. Palmer explained, a good doctor should have two or three years of medical school as well.

Daniel said he understood and was prepared to do what was necessary. Then he asked his most difficult question: Would Dr. Palmer be willing to take him on as an assistant, so that he could begin to learn medicine?

Dr. Palmer agreed, and in the spring of 1878, at the age of twenty-two, Daniel began his study of medicine. He soon found that medical books were much more interesting to him than law books had been. And he was very thankful he had studied German and Latin at the academy, for these languages helped him to understand difficult medical terms.

Dan and Dr. Palmer's other assistants, James Mills and Frank Pember, drove the buggy when the doctor visited his patients, kept his office in good order, and took care of his accounts. Little by little, the doctor taught them to make simple incisions, bandage cleanly, make plaster casts, set broken bones, and deliver babies safely, even in backwoods cabins under poor sanitary conditions.

In those days, there were few instruments such as thermometers to help a doctor diagnose an illness. Dr. Palmer showed the young men how a good physician could diagnose a disease by close observation and then use his experience to decide on the correct method of treatment.

Like other surgeons of the time, Dr. Palmer did almost no internal surgery. Rather, he did mostly emergency work: stitching up wounds, setting broken bones, or amputating toes, fingers, legs, or arms when injury was severe. Daniel assisted in all this.

After two years of such work, Dr. Palmer's three young assistants were ready for formal study. The doctor strongly advised that they go to Chicago Medical College, one of the best medical schools in the country. It had a solid three-year course of study—one year longer than that of most medical schools.

All three of Dr. Palmer's assistants passed the entrance examination for Chicago Medical College and were accepted for medical school. Daniel now faced a problem: how to pay for his school tuition, books, and laboratory fees, as well as for a room, food, and clothing for three years.

Harry Anderson, proud of Dan's accomplishments, helped him. First, Anderson got extra work for Daniel stringing wires for the new electrical and telephone services that were just coming to Janesville. Then the man who had become almost a father to Daniel helped him get a bank loan, which Anderson guaranteed, to pay for most of Daniel's school costs.

There remained only living expenses to worry about. Daniel wrote to his mother, asking for help. Her parents had recently died, and she had inherited part of their estate. Daniel was sure she could use some of it to help him. With this hope, Dan was off to Chicago, the proud owner of a new mustache and a new suit.

Daniel had already written to a family friend, Mrs. John Jones, a widow whose husband had worked with Daniel's father in the struggle for

Negroes' rights. Mr. Jones, a tailor who had grown wealthy from smart real estate investments, had been a respected member of Chicago's black community and was also highly thought of among the city's white population.

In Chicago, Daniel called at the house where Mrs. Jones lived with her daughters and granddaughter. It was a comfortable home not far from Chicago Medical College. Mrs. Jones, who had never had a paying boarder before, had an elegant and gentle manner. After a long talk, she told Dan that the son of her old friends would be welcome to stay. Mrs. Jones became a good friend to Daniel, introducing him to many of the leading African-American citizens of Chicago.

Daniel wrote to the Andersons: "I am faring better and have cheaper board than any student in the college . . . . Mrs. Jones . . . gave me a nice room, bath tub, gas, heat and 1st class board . . . . She charges me $3.75, which I think is very reasonable. Do you?"

By this time, Daniel had heard from his mother that she could not afford to send him any money. He wrote to Harry Anderson to thank him for his past help and "fatherly interest in me." Knowing that he would need to ask the kindly man for more financial aid, Daniel assured Anderson: "I keep account of my expenses and will render you account from time to time."

In another letter to Anderson, Dan wrote: "You

ask me if I made arrangements with Mrs. Jones to pay her . . . . I did not dare tell her I was so poor."

Daniel's letters home to the Andersons also described Chicago Medical College. The doctors, Dan wrote, wore formal black coats in the classrooms. In the operating rooms, they tied oiled silk aprons over these frock coats, which were double-breasted and knee-length. Everyone else in the operating room wore street clothes, too, for the practice of asepsis—keeping things clean and sterile near open wounds—was just beginning when Dan entered medical school.

Microscopes were also new. Daniel was excited to be able to see the germs that were the cause of infectious diseases. The labs and instruments were exciting to students who had worked with doctors like Henry Palmer—doctors who had to rely entirely on their own experience, observations, and instincts to diagnose illnesses.

Although he was the only black at the medical school, Dan Williams reported to the Andersons that he found no barriers because of his race. He was accepted by his teachers and friends with all the students. Still, he did not find medical school easy. He had thousands of facts to memorize and many techniques to learn.

Dan worked hard. He started out well, but his constant worry about money and a bad illness near the end of the school year meant he had to struggle in

Chicago Medical School, about 1880

his first year just to pass. He did better in his second and third years.

During Dan's years in medical school, advances in germ control, anesthetics, and drugs to fight infection finally allowed surgeons to begin to try internal surgery. Since germs could not be seen with the naked eye, some older doctors had trouble understanding the difference between ordinary household "clean" and absolute sterility. When operating, they refused to wear the new sterile gowns. If another doctor came into the operating room to observe or consult, the surgeon might shake his hand and then go right on with his operation. The students had the task of reminding the surgeon that he must disinfect his hands again.

Dan's favorite subject was anatomy, which dealt with the systems inside the human body. He wrote to Harry Anderson saying: "We all go to Dead house [morgue] where there assemble from fifty to one hundred doctors and everything is opened before us and understood."

Perhaps Daniel's interest in surgery followed from his interest in anatomy, or from having worked with Dr. Palmer, a fine surgeon for his time. Perhaps it grew out of his long years as a barber. A barber makes many quick decisions as he works. He must handle his tools confidently and surely. In fact, barbers were the first surgeons. Today their red-and-white poles—the colors of blood and bandages—are a reminder of their early occupation.

Daniel's money problems continued throughout his time in medical school. Dan did not want to take a part-time job, because he felt he needed all of his time for studying. So, almost each month when the money to Mrs. Jones was due, Dan would write to Harry Anderson. And each month, Anderson, whose business was now poor and who himself was struggling to care for his own large family, would scrape together the needed funds to send to the medical student who was so dear to him.

Dan's return to Janesville and the barbershop between his first and second years of medical school helped a little. But Dan was still recovering from his illness and unable to earn, or save, very much. And between his second and third years, Dan jumped at the chance to work—at no pay—at Mercy Hospital in Philadelphia. His job was to push dressing boxes from bed to bed and constantly change dressings for surgical patients, in order to minimize the chance of infection. He was also given the chance to do minor operations. The job was a mixed blessing. It gave Dan important experience, but it also made his financial needs even greater.

Because of the summer without pay, Daniel began his final year seriously short of money. Although he was now almost a member of Mrs. Jones's family—one of her grandchildren was his godchild—

he never told her about his severe financial condition.

Harry Anderson certainly did not have cash to spare, but again Daniel wrote him in desperation, "It is my final struggle for an education, and while I am at work I can't spare the time to go seek here and there for money to pay my living expenses." Dan asked Anderson to take out a bank loan. He promised, "You will get your money back and interest thereon." Once again his good friend came to his aid, and Daniel Hale Williams was able to graduate as a doctor in March of 1883.

4

Dining Room Operations

After Daniel Williams graduated from medical school, racial prejudice began to play a greater role in the choices he was able to make about his life. Following medical school, young doctors often worked in hospitals as interns. Being responsible for some of the day-to-day care of patients and helping the older doctors was a good way to learn more about the practice of medicine. However, internships were scarce, particularly for young black doctors. Williams discovered that no Chicago hospital would accept a black doctor on its staff. His summer work at Mercy Hospital turned out to be Williams's only internship.

Williams had thought he might want to set up practice in Washington, D.C. He went to visit the nation's capital but, in the end, decided to stay in

Chicago. "The real challenge is here," he wrote to his mother, who was living in Annapolis, Maryland. "Our Negro population is growing by leaps and bounds. We've already more than ten thousand blacks coming here to seek new freedoms and futures of opportunity."

Dr. Williams opened his medical practice in the area where he had lived with the Jones family—an integrated, well-to-do neighborhood. He was an able, confident doctor, and he soon had many patients, both black and white. Some of the first patients were Mrs. Jones's friends, who had known him as a student. Instead of calling him "Dr. Williams," they began calling him "Dr. Dan." The nickname would stick with him for the rest of his life.

Even after opening his own office, the young doctor remained interested in broadening his knowledge and keeping up with the latest in medical theory and practice. When great doctors from Europe visited, Daniel eagerly signed up for their courses. In 1887 he attended the International Medical Congress, where the latest medical findings were argued between doctors who clung to traditional methods and those who advocated scientific advances in medicine. Dan also continued his professional contacts with both his teachers and fellow students from medical school.

One of his former professors got him the job of physician at the Protestant Orphan Asylum, a

Dr. Dan began his practice in Chicago,
on a street like this one

position that paid nothing but provided wonderful experience and prestige. Dan had his hands full the year almost all of the 250 children came down with the measles at once!

But Dr. Dan's real interest was surgery. He continued to study anatomy by dissecting corpses, and the increasing number of successful operations he performed was gaining him a reputation as an excellent surgeon.

In the 1890s, many people distrusted hospitals, which were often viewed as places to die rather than to get well. In addition, African Americans could only be admitted to the large, crowded charity wards of hospitals, not to the smaller, more comfortable rooms. And because there were so few hospitals, many doctors were not able to associate with a hospital where they could admit patients for surgery. For all these reasons, most doctors used their own offices or, more often, patients' homes when they needed to operate. Many of the younger doctors, including Dr. Dan, ordinarily operated on Sunday mornings, when they did not have office hours. Medical colleagues served as each other's anesthetists, advisors, and assistants.

Before operating, Dr. Williams would prepare the home for the operation. Usually the dining room or kitchen was used because it held a large table. Some people were insulted by his hours of scrubbing their floor, walls, and ceiling. They thought their home already *was* clean.

With the patient's family, Dr. Dan sometimes even painted the room first, to be absolutely sure it was clean. He prepared sterile sheets for the patient to lie on by baking them in the oven. He sterilized instruments by boiling them on the stove. Before and during the operation, the air was sprayed with carbolic acid, a strong germ killer.

All this care was rewarded. Dr. Williams's patients rarely developed infections, and they usually recovered.

Dr. Williams's reputation as a highly skilled and successful surgeon spread, and he was appointed to the surgical staff of the South Side Dispensary, where he performed minor operations and demonstrated anatomy and surgical techniques for students at Chicago Medical College. He was also appointed surgeon for the City Railway Company—he was the first African American to be offered that position— and served as an expert medical witness when accident cases were on trial. Dr. Dan's name was becoming recognized in medical circles.

In 1889, Dr. Williams was appointed to the Illinois State Board of Health, another unpaid but highly prestigious position. The board was responsible for water safety and for sanitation in schools and restaurants. The board also was supposed to set medical standards.

In the late nineteenth century, many "quacks" without medical education roamed the country selling "medicines" that claimed to cure almost everything. Dr. Williams felt strongly that these phonies were a danger to the public—perhaps especially to poor African Americans from the rural South who were flooding Chicago in search of jobs. "There is no telling how many people these men have killed with their ignorance," Dr. Williams declared. "We've got to have state examinations for doctors; we've got to have state-approved medical schools; we've got to decide what we think a doctor should be able to do before we permit him to have a state license to practice medicine." Dr. Dan's standards were high, and he felt the public needed to be protected from "medicine" that did not heal.

At five feet eight inches tall, with his handsome face, well-proportioned body, and gentle manner, the young doctor who was so concerned about all people made an elegant figure walking through his neighborhood. His name was often in the African-American newspapers now, and he was a popular guest in Chicago's black society. He began to invest in real estate and was sought out for advice on business and careers.

While visiting an old friend in Albany, New York, Dr. Dan met Kittie May Blake, a light-skinned young woman with an excellent education and, like

Dr. Dan, a mixture of African and European ancestors. Daniel and Kittie May fell in love, he proposed marriage, and she accepted. Her mother, however, didn't want Kittie to marry a man associated with "colored people." A few years passed and Dan heard that Kittie had married a white lawyer. "His heart was broken," a friend later said.

Dan always kept in close touch with the Andersons, his adopted family. He visited them when he could. After both Ellen Anderson and one of her daughters died, Dan encouraged the remaining Andersons to move to Chicago. There Harry Anderson gave up barbering to work on his musical road shows. His daughter Traviata married a tenor in the musical group, Charles Bentley. Charles and Traviata were close friends of Daniel's, and the doctor often visited their home. Bentley later went to dental school and became a colleague of Dan's.

Dr. Daniel Hale Williams had started out well, but he felt he could always do better. He worked constantly to improve his medical skills.

5

Provident Hospital

When Dr. Williams was thirty-four years old, he had had his own practice for seven years. He was gaining recognition among both blacks and whites as an excellent doctor and surgeon. But almost daily he was reminded that, in the medical profession, racial prejudice remained a barrier to African Americans.

Daniel Hale Williams, despite his recognized skills, still could not admit his patients into a hospital in which he could operate on them. Further, those of his patients who were African-American could only be admitted to the charity wards of those hospitals. In addition, few black medical school graduates could find internships in hospitals. And most of the training courses that were being established for nurses, now that scientific medicine required skilled nursing care, were not open to African Americans.

Dan's concerns about the situation came clearly into focus one winter day in 1890. The Reverend Louis

Reynolds had asked Dr. Williams to come meet his sister, Emma. She had come to Chicago to study nursing, but none of Chicago's nursing schools would accept her as a student. The Reverend wondered if Dr. Williams, with his wide contacts, could help Emma find a place to study.

Williams thought hard before he answered. He had known for a long time that young African-American women needed access to good training as nurses. Young black doctors needed access to internships. Dr. Williams's patients needed access to good hospital treatment. He himself needed access to a hospital operating room.

Dr. Dan told Reverend Reynolds that instead of trying to find a place for Emma in an existing school, they would start their own hospital. For the first time in the United States, Williams said, young black women would be trained in up-to-date methods of nursing.

Work on making Dr. Dan's dream hospital a reality began at once. It soon seemed that all of Chicago rallied around the cause. Williams contacted his friends throughout the black community and throughout the white medical community. The respect in which he was held, as a doctor, a surgeon, and a man, made most people eager to help.

Committees supported each part of the effort: fund-raising, planning, collecting equipment, finding a building, choosing staff. Dr. Williams went to meeting after meeting, organizing and enthusiastically promoting the hospital, which he chose to call "Provident." Williams insisted on several points: The hospital would have the highest standards both for staff and for care. Also, although the hospital was to be founded so that blacks could come freely, it would be an interracial hospital, for patients and for staff.

Some African Americans did oppose the new hospital. They felt that establishing a separate hospital for blacks would only lead to more racial segregation. Dr. Williams argued that blacks could not afford to wait for whites to allow them good and equal hospital and training facilities. Instead, he said, African Americans should create these facilities for themselves.

For the most part, the community responded to the idea of a new hospital with a wave of enthusiasm. Wealthy citizens, both black and white, gave large sums of money. Smaller amounts were raised at church suppers, bazaars, and rallies. Children gave pennies at Sunday schools.

The hospital that came into being would not be familiar to anyone used to today's huge buildings with their modern equipment. Provident Hospital was established in an ordinary, three-story building that had been renovated, cleaned, painted, and furnished with donated equipment and furniture. There were beds for twelve patients, and a small operating room.

Sheets, towels, chairs, stoves, even beds were gifts. People who couldn't contribute money or large items donated everything from soap to jelly to home-baked bread for the hospital kitchen. One street vendor brought the vegetables he hadn't sold to the hospital at the end of each day. Even the material for the nurses' caps was donated.

Dr. Williams and the hospital board chose the staff carefully, keeping in mind the high standards that Daniel Williams had always considered important. Dr. Dan's friendships throughout the medical community brought some of the best white doctors in Chicago to Provident's staff. Among them were several of Daniel's former teachers from Chicago Medical College. One of these, Christian Fenger, a famous Danish surgeon who had become a good friend, helped establish the strict rules and practices for sanitation which the new hospital would follow.

Finding qualified black doctors was a more difficult task. Many African-American doctors had not been able to get the high-quality medical education that Dr. Williams considered necessary, not only for the sake of the patients, but because he wanted to show that a black-led institution could give the best possible care. Charles Bentley, husband of Harry Anderson's daughter, and now a dental surgeon of great skill, was an eminently qualified black staff member. Williams was also pleased to announce the appointment of Dr. Allen Wesley, a distinguished physician and former professor at Fisk University. But Dr. Dan rejected applications from several African Americans because he felt their qualifications were not good enough.

The search for nursing students was also more difficult than Dr. Williams had imagined. Dr. Dan had hoped that every student would have a high school diploma. However, education for African Americans was so poor at that time that few black women finished high school. And because nursing was looked on as simply an extension of family care, those women who had a high school education often had grander plans for their futures than to become nurses.

Dr. Williams wrote to urge people all around the country to tell the bright young women they knew about this opportunity for professional training. He knew that well-trained nurses were in demand to carry out the strict anti-infection procedures being introduced in hospitals everywhere. Finally, seven out of approximately two hundred applicants were chosen for the first nursing school class at Provident. Emma Reynolds was one of them.

About a year and a half after Dr. Dan first talked about his dream with Reverend Reynolds, Provident Hospital opened its doors on May 4, 1891.

The new hospital soon gained a reputation for giving excellent care. In the first year, 189 patients

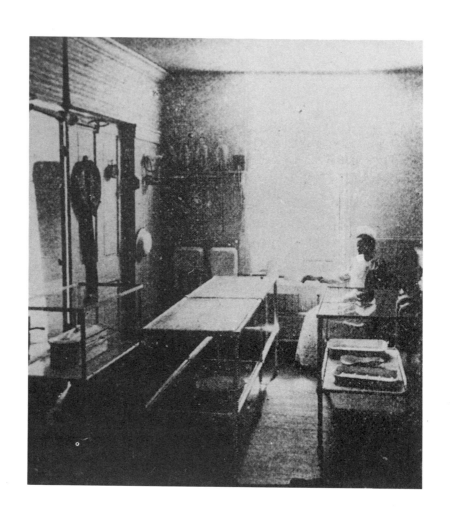

The operating room at Provident Hospital

were treated. Of these, 141 recovered completely, 23 showed some improvement, 3 showed no improvement, and 22 died—a very good record for a new hospital in the late nineteenth century.

Two problems that existed when Provident opened were to last the whole time Dr. Williams worked at the hospital. One was simply paying the bills. It was hard to keep the hospital going, particularly when many patients could not pay the full cost of their care. Funds needed to be raised continually.

In 1893, fund-raising became more difficult, for the United States was going through hard times. Although the hospital had already outgrown its small building, a move had to be postponed. Still the little hospital hung on, like a patient with a strong will to live and a good doctor.

Despite the hard times, Chicago held a World's Fair in 1893. Among the visitors to the city were Williams's sisters and his mother's cousin, Frederick Douglass, the runaway slave, abolitionist, writer, and government minister. At seventy-six, Douglass was a great hero to many people. After his appearance at the fair, Douglass spoke in a church, urging blacks to support Provident Hospital. Afterwards, he took more than $50 that had been collected and carried it himself to Provident, where a huge crowd had gathered to see him.

The second lasting problem that was to plague

the hospital and Dr. Daniel Williams was Dr. George Hall. When Dr. Hall, a black, had applied to be on the Provident staff, Dr. Dan had thought Hall did not meet the hospital's high standards. Hall's medical degree was from a school of poor quality. However, Hall had many friends who spoke for him, and the board finally persuaded Williams to accept him.

George Hall later received another medical degree, erasing doubts about his academic record. However, he never erased Williams's doubts about his professional qualifications. Dr. Hall, for his part, never forgot—or forgave—that Dr. Williams had opposed his joining the Provident Hospital staff.

Making an enemy of Dr. Hall was a major turning point in Daniel Williams's life. During his childhood, he had lived in a secure and happy family, and his father had been a kind advisor and teacher.

Later, though he was supporting himself and, for the most part, making his own choices about what he would do, Daniel Williams had found friends who helped him on his way. Harry Anderson took him into his home, gave him work, and helped support him in his studies. Dr. Palmer accepted him as an assistant and trained him. Mrs. Jones welcomed him as a boarder, then as a family friend.

But starting now, the smoldering fury of Dr. George Hall would affect even Dr. Williams's friendships and, eventually, change the very course of his life.

6

Surgical Skills

Just how well the young Provident Hospital was serving its patients could be seen in the operation to heal the knife wound in James Cornish's heart. This history-making operation was done in 1893, just two years after the hospital opened. Daniel Hale Williams did not operate alone. The staff must have developed high levels of skill, sanitation, and cooperation to have been able to support the world's first successful surgery on the heart.

The operation also showed Dr. Williams's excellence as a surgeon. During the years of his busy practice and community responsibilities—and even when he was creating, then running Provident—Dr. Dan made sure he kept up with the latest advances in medicine. He read medical journals to learn what new discoveries were being made in Europe. He took courses and attended lectures. At one point, he even took an extended leave of absence from his practice and returned to Chicago Medical College to study bacteriology.

But Williams, performing more and more operations, was most interested in the advances being made in internal surgery. He signed on to work at a local clinic to learn from a surgeon famous for his abdominal and pelvic operations. And, although he continued to serve his patients as a general family doctor, he gradually made surgery his specialty.

Williams had gone to the International Medical Congress in Washington, D.C., years before he operated on Cornish. There he had participated in lively debates between conservative doctors, who hesitated to cut into a patient, and the "new school" of surgeons, who argued that surgery did not have to result in infection if proper sanitation was used. Before sanitary techniques became commonly used, rates for surgical infection and death were high—about 90 percent of all surgical cuts into the body became infected. And most of the patients who contracted infections died. It was no wonder that the conservatives were afraid to operate!

Daniel Williams, who had become convinced of the importance of sanitation in surgery when still in medical school, was bolder than many doctors in deciding to operate. He believed that if a doctor delayed the operation too long, the patient might die before the operation.

Despite all the advances that had recently been made, surgical practice in the 1890s was, by today's standards, still primitive. A surgeon who dared open the chest or the stomach area had to be able to decide quickly what to do once he got inside, whatever he discovered there—and he had to do it without hesitation. Equipment was limited. The great infection-fighting drugs like penicillin had yet to be discovered. When blood was lost in surgery, there were no transfusions available to replace it. Anesthetics were crude and could not be given precisely. There were no X-rays to prepare the surgeon for what he would find inside the body he was about to enter and no heart-lung machines to keep the blood circulating during surgery.

Under these conditions, it was Dr. Williams's thorough knowledge of anatomy, together with his careful study of the medical history of each case, that gave him the confidence to take chances and the ability to make good decisions rapidly. As a surgeon, Dr. Dan was sure and swift, and known for his daring in what was still largely unknown territory.

Certainly Williams could not be sure what would happen when he followed James Cornish's knife wound deeper and deeper into his chest. Describing what he saw to the others in the room as he worked, Dr. Dan cut swiftly, but carefully. In the words of the report that Williams wrote later, the "wound was lengthened to the right, second incision was made from the centre of the first, carried over the middle of the cartilage and fifth rib about six inches in length. Sternum [breastbone], cartilage, and about one inch of the fifth rib were exposed."

The opening the surgeon cut into Cornish's chest was one and one-half inches across and two inches long. Through it, Williams could see muscles and blood vessels, including a large artery that had been bleeding. He cut or tied these structures off so he could work on the area beneath.

Soon Dr. Williams was able to see the pericardium. This protective sac encloses the heart as well as the arteries and veins as they approach the heart. The knife wound had cut through the pericardium and into the heart itself. Williams wrote: "A small punctured wound of the heart, about one-tenth of an inch in length, and about one-half of an inch to the right of the right coronary artery was seen."

The cut in the heart was small and not deep. Dr. Williams decided not to try to sew it up. The heart would heal itself.

Dr. Dan had to mend the gash in the pericardium, however, to help prevent infection or bleeding from reaching the heart. The pericardium moves with every heartbeat, and Cornish's heart was beating rapidly. Stitching the pericardium would be something like sewing the hand of a drummer as he plays.

First, Dr. Williams bathed the wound with a warm solution of salt water to help prevent infection. Then, holding the edges of the ripped pericardium with forceps, he sewed the edges together with his other hand.

Once the pericardium was mended, Williams reversed his passage, now moving back out of the chest. He sewed the ribs back to the sternum, then finished by closing the wound in the skin.

After the operation, Dr. Williams stayed close to his patient. "First twenty-four hours: Highest temperature, 103°F . . . . pulse, 130 . . . some pain in the region of the wound; slept six hours . . . . " said Williams's report.

James Cornish recovered smoothly. There was no severe bleeding and no infection. Several weeks after the original surgery, Williams reopened Cornish's chest to drain fluid that had collected there. Then, fifty-one days after the historic operation, Cornish walked out of Provident Hospital.

The response from the medical community and the public to what had taken place so calmly and quietly in the small operating room was loud and enthusiastic. The headline in one Chicago newspaper screamed, "Sews Up His Heart!" While Dr. Williams had not, technically, sewn up the heart itself, he had successfully entered and explored the heart region and surgically done what was necessary to save his patient's life.

A few months later, James Cornish returned to Provident Hospital. Apparently drunk and injured from another fight, he roared, "Where's Dr. Dan? I got to see Dr. Dan!" At first, Dr. Williams sternly told Cornish he wasn't worth saving. Then he appeared to relent, telling Cornish he had too much good surgery in him to let him die now. In fact, Cornish didn't die until 1943. He outlived Dr. Williams.

Some time later, certain people suggested that a European doctor had been the first to operate on the heart. Daniel Hale Williams seemed to take little interest in the question of who had been first. Dr. Williams knew that while he had saved one patient one day, there were more to be helped the next, and more the day after that. Not till almost four years after Cornish's surgery did Williams get around to writing his account of the operation for a medical journal.

The procedures and techniques Dan Williams had used in that historic operation soon became standard. Williams himself used them again, several times. Years later, he recreated the wound, then reenacted the operation, on a dead body. He found that skin and the flesh near the body's surface will reclose tightly after a deep cut, which was why he had not, at first, been able to tell how serious Cornish's wound was.

7

Freedmen's Hospital

In 1894, Dr. Daniel Hale Williams was appointed surgeon-in-chief, or head, of Freedmen's Hospital in Washington, D.C. A new president, Grover Cleveland, had been elected and was filling top jobs throughout the government. The new secretary of state, Judge Walter Gresham of Chicago, was on the advisory board of Provident Hospital. He had urged Williams to apply for the job.

Provident was ending its third year with a sound financial base and a good staff. The job at Freedmen's would be a great challenge for Williams: While Provident had twelve beds, Freedmen's had two hundred.

The Washington hospital had originally been part of the Freedmen's Bureau Asylum and Refugee Camp, established after the Civil War. Many ex-slaves moved to the nation's capital during and after the war. The bureau's job was to help them make new and productive lives.

Freedmen's in 1894 was in many ways a local hospital, yet it was supervised by the U.S. Department of the Interior. Some of its staff, buildings, and labs were shared with Howard University Medical School. All these connections made Freedmen's Hospital complicated to lead.

Although Dr. Williams was appointed at the end of February and sworn in, he did not start work at Freedmen's until fall. On what was to have been his last weekend in Chicago, he went hunting with friends and was accidentally shot in the right foot. An infection started, and it quickly spread from the foot to the leg.

The wound did not heal well, and Dr. Dan proved himself a poor patient. Eager to get to Washington, he kept getting up and trying to work before he should have. Finally, when it seemed that Williams's leg must be amputated, he put himself under the care of Dr. Christian Fenger, his old teacher and friend, who was on the Provident staff. With six months' worth of patience and excellent care, Dr. Fenger managed to save Daniel Williams's leg.

Always afterwards, Williams reminded doctors that an arm or a leg was part of a person who needed it, a person who had to work for a living. Doctors must, if at all possible, he said, keep the body whole. Williams thought a decision to amputate was often made from impatience, or to hide incompetence.

During the delay in getting to Washington, Williams was the victim of several vicious verbal attacks. Dr. George Hall, still angry that Dr. Williams had judged Hall unfit for the staff at Provident, wrote to a Washington newspaper, saying Williams would never be able to take over at Freedmen's. Then Hall had a friend write to the Interior Department, claiming that while Williams was supposedly ill and collecting a government salary, he was actually well and working at Provident. These charges had little effect, but they were a sample of what lay ahead.

When Williams finally moved to Washington, he was no longer elegantly slim but thin and frail. He lived at first in a house he had bought for his mother and two sisters. Later he moved into an apartment at the hospital.

Dr. Williams found he had a great deal to do at Freedmen's. The wooden frame buildings, built for temporary use long before, were in poor condition. Each was heated by a single stove. Surgery patients were wheeled from one building to another for their operations, in any weather. The kitchen was in a separate building. Patients who could walk were forced to go outside to get their meals. Meals for bedridden patients were usually delivered cold.

In the wards, patients were jumbled together, not grouped according to their illnesses. Patients did much of what little cleaning was done. Williams was shocked by the way medicine was given out. Every hour, a nurse called out the time. Then the patients, no matter how sick or confused, were expected to dose themselves, if medicine was due. The nursing staff was small and completely untrained.

Cleansing procedures were not taken seriously. Most operations were still done by staff wearing ordinary clothes, with no masks and no rubber gloves. The death rate was alarmingly high.

The financial situation at Freedmen's was also bad. Williams had to deal with strict government budgets and to compete for funds with other agencies. He quickly found he just did not have the money to run a good hospital.

Faced with these obstacles, Dr. Dan immediately dug into his job. He began with reforms that cost little, grouping staff and buildings into departments, and patients according to their illnesses. Surgical patients were placed into the same building as the operating room. Dr. Dan also had flowers planted on the grounds so patients could see them on their walks and so cut flowers could be brought indoors to brighten the drab, ramshackle buildings.

Soon Dr. Williams introduced modern techniques for examining specimens and tissue samples, so doctors would have as much information as possible about a patient before beginning treatment. Then he recruited an interracial staff of twenty of Washington's best doctors to serve as unpaid consultants, giving some black doctors their first opportunity to be associated with a hospital. And as he had done at Provident Hospital, Dr. Williams set up a system of internships to supplement the staff of twenty doctors. He reasoned that such a move would save money by doing away with the need for paid medical assistants and would also offer young African-American medical school graduates the training that was still denied them in most American hospitals.

Dr. Dan wanted to make Freedmen's a national center for the training of black nurses, so he established a school for nurses patterned on the one he had started at Provident. The standards set for the student nurses were high. But Dr. Williams was confident that carefully selected students rigorously trained in hygiene and nursing skills would help bring down Freedmen's death rate.

To direct the nursing program, he hired Sarah Ebersole, an excellent surgical nurse and administrator from Chicago. By 1895, thirty-seven students from many states were hard at work. They lived in a dormitory on the grounds and were paid five dollars a month to cover expenses.

Because Freedmen's had been an inferior hospital for so long, it had become known as a hospital to which only African Americans who could not afford better care went. Once the hospital began to improve, Dr. Dan set about encouraging middle-class blacks to use it. One method he used was to make some of the demonstration operations for students open to the public. On Sunday afternoons, people could come and watch Dr. Dan and other surgeons operate. People could see for themselves the high quality of the medical care available from black doctors at Freedmen's. Slowly Freedmen's reputation began to improve.

Doctoring and running the hospital, though difficult tasks, were familiar to Dr. Williams. But what was less familiar about his work at Freedmen's—the political aspects of his job—gave him serious trouble. Daniel Williams was responsible to several different government bodies, and their budget officers, for the hospital's progress. He often had to fight for the funds he needed to do a good job. Williams had to deal with jealousy and opposition at Howard Medical College, which had had a poor nursing program before he started his excellent one.

Dr. Williams even found competition inside Freedmen's itself. Dr. Charles B. Purvis, Freedmen's previous surgeon-in-chief, had been the first black civilian in the United States to head a hospital. Purvis had fought to keep his job. Although he had lost out to Williams, Purvis remained on the staff, angry and with considerable power.

Once, when he was discouraged by the pressures

**Dr. Williams with nursing students
at Freedmen's Hospital, about 1897**

on him, Dr. Williams went to visit Frederick Douglass and told him of the difficulties he was facing. Douglass responded:

> *My boy, you say you see what ought to be done. Well, hoping will do no good, now or any time. There is only one way you can succeed, Dan, and that is to override the obstacles in your way. By the power that is within you, my boy, do what you hope to do.*

Daniel Williams quoted these encouraging words years later to other blacks who were trying to gain the courage to take a great step for themselves.

Despite the political problems, Dr. Williams's work as a surgeon remained satisfying. He performed some of his most famous operations while at Freedmen's. Many of these would today be done by specialists: operations on the brain, heart, abdomen, ovaries, and womb.

One night at the opera, Williams met a boy of thirteen who hoped to be a violinist. The boy had a growth on his wrist. He was afraid an operation would damage the nerves in his arm, and he would no longer be able to play. Dr. Dan assured him that his would be a minor operation. The boy and his parents agreed that Dr. Williams could operate, and the wrist healed without complications.

Operations that required Dr. Dan to probe inside

a body, to remove a tumor or to aid in a difficult birth, were more complex. Dr. Williams would hold his audience of students and doctors spellbound as he met, then mastered, one problem after another.

One famous operation began as the removal of an eighteen-pound tumor from the abdomen of a pregnant woman. The baby was safe, but Dr. Williams discovered so many more tumors that he finally had to deliver the child prematurely. The situation became even more complex as Dr. Williams, lecturing as he dealt with each new complication, found many other tumors. In the end, he decided to remove the woman's uterus.

Doctors came from all around Washington to watch Daniel Williams operate and to bring him their most difficult cases. Although white doctors were among those who came, and although his cases were discussed at the District of Columbia Medical Society, Dr. Williams was not invited to join or even to visit the society. Dr. Dan missed the professional discussions and exchanges of experience he had enjoyed in Chicago, where he was the member of several medical societies. In 1895, he helped to establish a medical society that had both black and white members. That same year, Williams also helped form, and became vice president of, the National Negro Medical Association of Physicians, Surgeons, Dentists and Pharmacists. The same organization, now called the National

Medical Association, exists today.

Daniel Williams had both good times and bad in his personal life during the years he worked in Washington. Frederick Douglass's death in February 1895 began a tragic series. Traviata Anderson, Harry's daughter and Dr. Charles Bentley's wife, died. Dr. Henry Palmer, who had given Dan his start in medicine, and Judge Gresham, Daniel's sponsor for the job at Freedmen's, both died. Finally, Dan's brother, Price, the successful Philadelphia lawyer, died unexpectedly. He was buried in Annapolis beside their father.

Just turning forty, Dr. Williams was a handsome, famous man—and unmarried. Naturally, he was popular and was often invited to parties in the black community. At one of these parties he met the beautiful woman he would marry.

Alice Johnson was the daughter of a white man, Moses Jacob Ezekiel, and a light-skinned black woman, Isabella Johnson, who had worked as a seamstress for the wealthy Ezekiel family in Richmond, Virginia. The Ezekiels were an Orthodox Jewish family, and Moses's father was an outspoken champion of Jewish rights. The family did not want Moses and Isabella to marry, and Virginia law did not then permit interracial marriage. In any case, Moses, who wanted to be an artist, had no money to support a family. He went off to train for service in the Civil

War. During Moses's military service, Isabella gave birth to his daughter.

After the war, Moses moved to Europe to study sculpture. Isabella moved to Washington, where she supported her daughter by sewing. As Alice grew up, her father sent money and presents, and from time to time he visited. When Moses finally began to sell some pieces of sculpture—when Alice was seventeen and studying at Howard University to be a teacher— Moses sent for his childhood sweetheart and his daughter.

Alice and Isabella apparently expected to live with Moses from then on. But the women had lived independently for many years, and they found it hard to adjust to a foreign culture. They returned to the United States to live, though they stayed in touch with Moses.

When Dr. Dan met Alice, she was thirty-nine years old. A quiet, serious woman, she was much admired for her beauty. She had taught at Mott Elementary School for over twenty years and was now assistant principal there.

Alice and Dan often attended the same parties. And they enjoyed many of the same activities. William Warfield, a former intern who had been promoted to assistant surgeon at Freedmen's, had become Dan's close friend. The doctors often took Alice and her friend Caroline Parke driving in the countryside.

When Alice's mother became ill, Dan discovered that she had cancer. Mrs. Johnson didn't want to go to a hospital, so Dr. Dan operated on her in her home. But she could not be cured. As Mrs. Johnson lay dying, she begged Dr. Dan to care for Alice.

Six months later, Dan and Alice were married. Their courtship had been so quiet that all but their closest friends were surprised when they made the announcement. The young black poet Paul Laurence Dunbar, who had often been a patient at Freedmen's, had become a friend of Dan's. Dunbar wrote a long poem in celebration of the wedding. It began:

Step me now a bridal measure,
Work give way to love and leisure,
Hearts be free and hearts be gay—
Doctor Dan doth wed today.

By the time of his marriage, Daniel Hale Williams was ready to return to Chicago. In the four years he had been its head, he had turned Freedmen's into an excellent hospital. However, the political situation, both within the hospital and in the government, was growing worse.

Some people at Howard Medical College still held grudges against Dr. Williams. Dr. Purvis remained eager to get his old job back. President Cleveland had been defeated for reelection and the new

Alice Johnson, Mrs. Daniel Hale Williams

president was appointing his own people. The federal government was in a constant tug-of-war with the District of Columbia government about who was responsible for Freedmen's. Dr. Williams, who disliked infighting, found himself in a river with many currents. He had a hard time keeping afloat.

The crisis began in the spring of 1897. A congressional committee began to investigate the management of all charitable institutions in Washington, D.C. At issue for Freedmen's was whether the hospital should continue to be run by the Interior Department or be handed over to the District of Columbia government to manage. In addition, there were rumors that Dr. Williams had done some things that were irresponsible. Although he was not thinking of resigning, Williams was surprised and hurt to discover that an examination had been announced for people who wanted to become surgeon-in-chief.

Dr. Williams was unable to get an appointment with the secretary of the interior, whose department was in charge of Freedmen's, to find out what was happening. He went to see Senator James McMillan of Michigan, the chairman of the congressional committee. Dr. Williams gave a careful history of the mess he had found at Freedmen's and of what he had done to improve the situation.

Senator McMillan was impressed. He said he would speak to the interior secretary. A few weeks later it was announced that there was no vacancy for surgeon-in-chief at Freedmen's.

When the congressional hearing was finally held, Daniel Williams laid out his record and was cleared of all charges and free to go on with his work at Freedmen's. Instead, he resigned. He had done his job. Freedmen's Hospital was a respected institution. What was most needed now was a modern hospital building, and Williams knew that was not likely to be built soon. He chose to go back to Chicago and his beloved Provident.

Dan and Alice were soon on their way to Chicago. Within a few days in April 1898, Williams left Freedmen's, married, and left Washington with his bride.

8

Back to Chicago

Dr. Daniel Williams, returning to Chicago in 1898, could look forward to a bright future. His friends gave a huge welcoming party and wedding reception for him and Alice. Just over forty, Williams had decades of good work ahead. What's more, he and Alice planned to start a family.

All too soon, though, Dan found that he had not left politics behind when he left Washington. He had not even left Washington politics behind.

Within a few months, Dr. Williams had to return to Washington to defend himself in new hearings about Freedmen's Hospital. Because the congressional committee's report had recommended that control of Freedmen's be transferred from the national government to the local government, the Interior Department, in an attempt to remain in charge of the hospital, had issued its own report.

This report contained serious charges aimed at Williams, who was said to be a good surgeon but a poor manager who kept sloppy records.

Daniel Williams was accused of using hospital funds to buy books and medical instruments that he kept when he left the hospital. Another charge was that Dan sold as his own a camera that belonged to the hospital. Some of the complaints about the management of Freedmen's were problems Williams himself had actually reported earlier.

Dr. Williams appeared at the hearings and went down the list of charges one by one. He proved that he did own the camera in question by showing the receipt for its purchase. He explained that instruments are often broken during operations and must be replaced. Dan said he had left more books, including some of his own, at Freedmen's than he'd found there when he arrived. Once again, he was able to prove that the charges against him were false.

However, Dan Williams was saddened by the hearings. The charges had come in part from people who had been on his own staff. One was Dr. William Warfield, whom Dr. Dan had trained—the same young man who had joined in outings with him when Dr. Dan was courting Alice. Another was Sarah Ebersole, whom he had brought from Chicago to head the Freedmen's nursing school. Austin Curtis, who had succeeded Williams as head of Freedmen's, had also turned against him.

The pain of having people he had worked with and trusted turn on him was great. For many years, Daniel Williams refused to have any assistant, even a secretary, in his Chicago office.

Williams had private troubles as well. The year after they moved to Chicago, the baby he and Alice were expecting was born early and died. The doctor barely saved Alice's life, and afterwards she was unable to bear children. Williams's mother died the next year.

Trying to forget the sadness that now lay over his life, Williams went eagerly to work. He returned to his old practice and to Provident Hospital. In Dr. Williams's absence, Provident had not had an official head. So most of its staff and board warmly welcomed his return to his old position as chief surgeon of the hospital, which was now housed in a new sixty-five-bed building. In addition, Dr. Dan was pleased to find that other hospitals also were now eager to have him on their staffs. By 1900, he had patients—both black and white—in five hospitals at once.

Dr. Williams took on other work, too. He helped examine soldiers for the 8th Illinois Regiment, a black unit going off to fight in the Spanish-American War. He served on the staff of the Old Folks Home

Provident Hospital and Training School for Nurses

and renewed his connections with various medical societies.

But all was not well for Williams at his own hospital, though he may not have realized this at first, since he spent much of his time seeing patients in his office and at other hospitals. During Williams's years away in Washington, the management of Provident Hospital had been reorganized so that committees of board and staff members now handled its day-to-day operations. Williams's old enemy, Dr. George Hall, had become a member of both the board and many of these committees.

When Dr. Dan returned to Provident, Dan joined the committee where he felt he could do the most good: the fund-raising committee. He was not particularly interested in taking part in the daily running of the hospital. On the other hand, Dr. Hall was very active in the committees that made day-to-day decisions, and he found many ways to undercut Williams. Sometimes the operating room was not ready when Dr. Williams was scheduled to operate. At other times, he found that he did not have enough nursing help during surgery, or his patients complained that they were being rudely treated by the hospital staff.

It is not clear why George Hall stayed angry at Dan Williams for so long. Some people who have studied Williams's life suggest that one reason may have been that both Hall and his wife, who raised funds for the hospital, were dark-skinned blacks. Daniel Williams was a fair-skinned black, as was his wife. In addition, many of Dan and Alice's black friends were light-skinned. Mrs. Hall once called Williams a "fair complexioned fellow [who] doesn't quite seem to know what race he wants to belong to."

Williams's very light skin had caused him uneasiness in his professional life for some time. He had found that looking white while being black could lead to suspicion and prejudice on both sides of the color line. When he met white people for the first time, he found it awkward to mention that he was black, yet he didn't want to be thought of as trying to "pass" as white.

On the other hand, some African Americans, particularly those with very dark skins, felt Williams thought he was better than they because he looked white and had many colleagues in the white medical community. So the Halls found some sympathy when they suggested that Williams was turning his back on blacks.

In fact, Daniel Williams had always worked hard to make life better for African Americans. He commented on the meaning of lightness or darkness of skin in a paper he wrote. In the paper, Williams observed: "The color of the skin in this country furnishes no correct index of the purity of the blood of a colored person any more than it does the purity of the blood of a white person." He asked "where the line is to be drawn" between the two races when in the same family were often found brothers and sisters of varied skin color—black, white, and in between—born of the same parents.

Despite the friction, for the most part Williams was so busy during his first years back in Chicago that he paid little attention to Hall and the problems at Provident. In 1908, Dr. Williams finally brought in an apprentice doctor, Ulysses Grant Dailey, to share his office and his workload.

Young Dailey found Williams somewhat fussy to work with but a patient teacher. Williams encouraged him to study continually: "Your answers can only be found in the dissecting room," he said once, and immediately took Dailey to examine a corpse in order to find the answer they were looking for.

One reason Williams needed an assistant was that he was doing more and more work away from Chicago. His reputation as a doctor was so great that patients traveled long distances to be treated by him. But he himself also traveled all over the country, giving lectures and demonstrating surgical techniques.

Sometimes African-American doctors in remote areas would gather their difficult cases, raise funds, and invite Williams to come, operate, and teach them. As in the old days, Dr. Dan operated and lectured in kitchens, dining rooms, and parlors—even outdoors when so many young black doctors wanted to learn from the great surgeon that the available room would not hold them all.

Dr. Williams also began to spend time helping to set up and improve black medical colleges and hospitals to train and support African-American doctors and nurses. His association with Meharry Medical College in Nashville, Tennessee, lasted many years.

Williams was delighted when officials at Meharry asked him to teach surgery and demonstrate operations for a week or ten days a year. Dr. Williams did as many as six or eight operations a day in the basement operating room, by lamp and candlelight. But he knew this situation was not good enough. If the white hospitals in the South would not accept black interns for training or teach black nurses or allow African-American doctors to practice, he insisted, "We must start our own hospitals and training schools!"

At a public meeting held to raise support for a black hospital in Nashville, Dr. Dan argued that every city in the South with a population of ten thousand black people should have a hospital and a training school for nurses. He pointed out: "Before the founding of Provident Hospital there was not in this country a single hospital or training school for nurses owned and managed by colored people . . . . [and] now there are twelve!"

Williams continued: "Our white friends cannot do for us what we can do for ourselves . . . . When we have learned to do well what we have the ability to do, we will have accomplished much towards changing sentiments now against us." The speech was widely distributed, and it inspired African Americans in Nashville and other black communities to start their own hospitals.

Dr. Williams followed up his inspiration and encouragement with help and practical advice. He drew on his experience at Provident, for instance, when he suggested that the Meharry hospital be started in a small house that was easy to keep clean. He established a library at Mercy Hospital. And he was always ready to come, operate, demonstrate, and lecture.

Despite his busy schedule and the fame his surgery was gaining for him, Williams always remembered that "cases" were about individual human lives. Once he was asked to examine a six-year-old boy who had fallen from a wagon. The boy's lower leg was so badly torn and infected that other doctors thought amputation would be necessary. But Dr. Williams remembered how Dr. Fenger had worked to give Dan's own leg time to heal itself rather than cutting it off.

After six months under Dr. Williams's care, the boy left the hospital, walking on his own two feet.

As Dr. Williams's reputation grew, Dr. Hall's feelings became more obvious and harmful. At a meeting of the National Medical Association in 1905, Williams demonstrated a difficult operation. Finding one complication after another, he described them all and the possible ways of dealing with them to the audience of doctors. At one point, Hall, who was sitting near the front, loudly challenged, "If it's too much for you, why don't you come out and close up?" Williams, who disliked public argument, immediately ended his teaching, quickly finished the operation, and silently left the room.

In 1908, a banquet was held to celebrate Dr. Daniel Williams's twenty-five years as a doctor. Physicians from all over the country sent gifts and good wishes. Chicago doctors presented Williams with a large silver bowl inscribed with a message of appreciation and their names. Dr. Hall's name was not on the bowl.

The final crisis between Williams and Hall came in 1912. Williams had been appointed associate attending surgeon on the staff of St. Luke's, one of Chicago's finest hospitals. This great honor not only helped Dr. Williams and his patients, it broke down still another barrier between the black and white medical communities.

Dr. Hall did not allow the Provident board to see the appointment in this way. Although Williams had had patients in primarily white hospitals for years, Hall now made a big point of the fact that most of St. Luke's patients were white and wealthy and accused Williams of "selling out the black race." "If he is serious about better health care for black people why doesn't he spend all of his time at Provident?" Hall asked.

Many of the doctors with whom Dr. Williams had worked at Provident in the old days had by now died or retired. There were few left to defend Dr. Dan's actions. In addition, Williams would not help himself by explaining how it would benefit Provident for him to work in hospitals throughout the city.

Many African Americans took Dr. Williams's silence to mean he had turned away from helping them. Chicago blacks divided into two camps. Even the Anderson family, even Dan's cousins, were divided in what they thought of him.

Soon Hall was able to persuade the Provident board to send Williams a letter saying he should bring all his patients to Provident. Again Dr. Williams made no comment. But this time he submitted his resignation. He cut all ties to Provident Hospital, the hospital he had worked so hard to establish twenty years before.

How could so skillful a person be defeated by Hall's tactics? One of Dr. Williams's colleagues once said, "After Dan Williams graduated in medicine, he never had another single interest in life. . . . So single-tracked was his mind he could not begin to cope with medicine politics. He had no stomach for a fight."

The years after he left Provident were busy and productive for Daniel Williams. He had plenty to do, as a doctor and as a teacher. He worked constantly to improve medical practices and to improve opportunities for African Americans, both as patients and as professionals.

Dr. Williams continued to work at Meharry and many other black medical and teaching institutions. He remained at St. Luke's until he retired from medicine. He remained an active member of Chicago medical societies and spoke at state and national meetings. When the American College of Surgeons was founded in 1913, Dan Williams was its only black charter member.

In 1920 Dan and Alice Williams built a summer and retirement home in beautiful Idlewild in the woods of northern Michigan. There Dr. Dan was able to forget his cares and enjoy his favorite sports—swimming, fishing, and hunting. Unfortunately, almost as soon as the lovely retreat was built, Alice contracted Parkinson's disease. Although she spent

Dr. Daniel Hale Williams, a leader in opening the field of medicine to African Americans

most of the next four years in a wheelchair, she never expressed sorrow or frustration at her fate. Alice kept busy reading and attending concerts until she died in 1924.

Then, in 1926, Daniel Williams had a stroke. Over the next five years, a series of additional strokes affected his mental ability and increasingly limited his activities. A niece came to care for him, and many people who knew what he had accomplished continued to honor him and to visit. But Dr. Dan's last years were sad and often lonely. Dr. Williams died in August of 1931.

Dr. Daniel Williams did not leave a large fortune. He provided for several people in his family: his sisters, his brother Price's widow, and the niece who had taken care of him. He made gifts to a number of employees and friends.

Beyond that, Williams left several gifts to support the work of his lifetime, extending his legacy to schools and hospitals that helped African Americans. He left money to Howard Medical College, the college associated with Freedmen's Hospital; to Meharry Medical College; and to a proposed new interracial hospital in Chicago. Any who still doubted his true commitment to blacks might have noticed that the largest sum Daniel Williams left was to the National Association for the Advancement of

Colored People.

Daniel Hale Williams, the son of a barber, was a great surgeon, the first ever to operate successfully on the human heart. He established the nation's first interracial hospital for the treatment of African-American patients and the training of black interns and black nurses. He contributed to the development of other excellent hospitals to serve the same needs and helped open up previously all-white hospitals both to African-American doctors and nurses, and to African-American patients. By the time Daniel Williams died, an entire generation of black doctors and nurses was working across the United States—a living testament to his teaching, guidance, and encouragement.

For Further Reading

Readers interested in learning more about the life of Daniel Hale Williams may want to read the following:

- *Daniel Hale Williams: Surgeon* by Flossie Thompson-Peters (Atlas Press, 1988).

- *Black Pioneers of Science & Invention* by Louis Haber. A chapter which covers Daniel Hale Williams is included (Harcourt Brace, 1970).

- *Great Black Americans* by Ben Richardson and William Fahey. Contains a chapter on Daniel Hale Williams in the section devoted to "Science" (HarperCollins, 1990).

- *11 African-American Doctors* edited by Robert C. Hayden. Includes a chapter on Daniel Hale Williams (Revised edition, Twenty-First Century Books, 1992).

Readers may also find these books about Daniel Hale Williams in their local library:

- *Daniel Hale Williams, Negro Surgeon* by Helen Buckler (Pitman Publishing, 1968).

- *Daniel Hale Williams: Open-Heart Doctor* by Lewis Federson (McGraw-Hill, 1971).

- *The Heart Man: Dr. Daniel Hale Williams* by Louise Meriwether (Prentice Hall, 1972).

- *Sure Hands, Strong Heart: The Life of Daniel Hale Williams* by Lillie Patterson (Abingdon, 1981).

INDEX

References to photographs are listed in *italic, **boldface*** type.